CYRIL DAVEY

MARTIN LUTHER

Hero of the Reformation

Hunt & Thorpe

In Australia this book is published by:
Hunt & Thorpe Australia Pty Ltd.
9 Euston Street, Rydalmere NSW 2116

Acknowledgments
Cephas Picture Library: 45.
Mary Evans Picture Library: cover, title page, 7, 9, 11, 12, 13, 15, 20, 22/23, 24,
    25, 28, 31, 32/33, 35, 36/37, 38, 41, 43, 46.
National Portrait Gallery: 4, 45.
Zefa Picture Library: 16, 17.

A CIP catalogue record for this book is available from the British Library.

Manufactured in U.K.

CONTENTS

Introduction

HERE I STAND!

The narrow streets of the German city of Worms were crowded with townspeople and peasants. So was the city square facing the Council House. This was where the "Diet," the emperor's Council, was meeting to decide what would happen to Martin Luther, the monk from Wittenberg. It was this monk, not the emperor, who the people wanted to see. He was their new hero.

They never saw him. He was hustled in by a side door. A plain-faced, brown-robed man, not quite forty years old, he stood in the council chamber before dukes and princes in their splendid dress, bishops and cardinals in scarlet and purple robes, the emperor himself, crowned, on a throne.

He was accused by the leaders of the Catholic Church for saying and writing that many of the things the Church did and taught were wrong – that even the Pope himself was often wrong. Now, before the emperor, he must admit that he himself was wrong, that Church and pope were right after all.

He stared round the great chamber, his hand on the girdle of his monk's robe. His words were clear and defiant.

"Here I stand! I can do no other. So help me God!"

He knew he could be killed for those words

It all happened nearly 500 years ago, but what Martin Luther said and did are as important today as ever.

1

THE FURNACE-MASTER

Hans Luther was a farmer's son who thought he could do better for himself than working from dawn to nightfall in the fields, and so he had gone to work instead in the coal mines at Eisleben, in Germany. Then, when he had made a good deal more money than he had on the farm, he became a furnace-master, melting iron and turning it into tools, ironwork for carts and houses, and so on. He did so well that he bought a second furnace, and then a third and a fourth.

Little Martin, his son, loved the red fiery glow of the furnace and grew up with the smell of the foundry on his father's clothes. He also grew up remembering his father's words.

"Our Martin is going to do better than this! He's going to be rich, and famous, and marry a pretty wife! No hard work for *him*! We'll send him to the university and make him a lawyer!" Then Hans would laugh and heave Martin onto his shoulder as his wife crossed the room and made the sign of the cross in front of the painted, wooden carving of St. Anne on the wall.

"St. Anne has looked after *us*, and she'll look after *him*!" she said. St. Anne, the mother of the Virgin Mary, was the patron saint of the Luther family, and so they prayed to her every day.

"He'll be famous – *and* rich, our Martin," shouted the furnace-master as he put his son down.

He was not quite correct. Martin would never be rich, though he would certainly be famous.

Hans (left) and Margarete, Luther's parents.

7

2

"OF COURSE THE EARTH IS FLAT!"

Most ordinary people in those days were *sure* the earth was flat –
if you sailed far enough you would fall over the edge. Martin was
only ten when Christopher Columbus proved them wrong by
sailing on and on, westward until he found a "new" land, which
was given the name of America. People's ideas of the world would
have to change.

Other things were changing, too. Printing had been invented
only some forty years before Martin Luther was born. Although
there were no books in school, books and pamphlets and leaflets
were on sale in all the towns – and written in German, too. That
was another change. Educated people all learned Latin so they
could talk to people from other countries who spoke different
languages. Church services were all in Latin, never understood by
peasants and workers who stood in the church and watched.
Would *that* ever change?

Christians in western Europe were Catholics, accepting and
believing whatever the Church and the priests said. The pope, in
Rome, was the head of the Church and no one could argue with
what *he* said. The pope was *always* right.

That, surely, could never change!

But a great many things *were* changing. The peasants
themselves were often in a rebellious mood, wanting to be treated
better than they were.

It was an exciting world to grow up in, but a frightening one,
too.

The house in Mohra in eastern
Germany, where in 1483 Martin Luther
was born.

3

THE BOY WHO MADE A PROMISE

Martin was very frightened indeed as he pushed his way through the woods and realized he was lost. The schoolmaster-priest said he was stupid and made him stand in front of his class at school wearing a donkey's-head mask. He had been beaten fourteen times in one week for doing his Latin badly – and beaten again by his father for being beaten in school. The only thing to do had been to run away, across the fields outside the town wall and into the thick woods. Now he was lost, and the farther he went the more lost he became. What terrified him were the awful "things" waiting for him – the witches and elves and demons his mother had told him lived among the trees.

Once when he was very little, he had even seen a devil himself – or so he believed. With other boys, he had been watching the sick people standing outside the great church waiting for the priest to come and bless them. Then, when the priest did so, Martin was sure he had seen a devil fly out of one man's mouth. He had run home to tell his mother.

He plunged on through the trees. It was no use praying to God – God would be angry, too, that he had been beaten. But St. Anne would help!

"Please, dear St. Anne, if you help me, I'll do whatever you want. I'll never run away again!"

Next morning a woodsman found him asleep under the bushes and took him home. Martin kept his word. He would often be scared, but he would never run away. He would always face whatever came with courage.

4
UNIVERSITY

Martin was a great deal more clever than the beatings for "doing badly in Latin" would suggest – so clever, indeed, that he had no difficulty in getting a place in the university at Erfurt. His father, Hans, never tired of boasting about him.

"We've made up our minds about his future. He's going to be a lawyer...a *famous* lawyer – and when he is he'll pay back all the money we've spent on sending him to school and university!"

Martin's friends felt the same way, and he had plenty of them. He may have been the most brilliant scholar in the university, but he was good company, too, especially when he played his lute and led them in their favorite songs after supper. But then, suddenly, when they asked him to play again he would be gone. He would slip off into the darkness to wander about the streets alone. The students would shrug their shoulders. "He's in one of his moods again!"

His "moods" came more frequently, and always because he wanted to please God but, at the same time, felt sure that God was angry with him. He thought that God would not forgive him because he did not say enough prayers, go to church more often, punish himself enough. It was wrong to enjoy himself with his friends, when he ought to have been saying prayers instead.

"I ought to be a monk, not a lawyer!" he said to himself grimly...and imagined what his father would say about *that* idea!

Luther in the library at Erfurt University, where in 1501, he went to study law and philosophy.

DATES

1483 Nov 10	Born	
1487	Began school at Mansfeld	Age 4

1495	Went to Magdeburg Cathedral School	Age 12
1497	St. George's Church School at Eisenach	Age 14
1501–1505	Studied at Erfurt University	Age 17–21
1505	Entered Augustinian Monastery, Erfurt	Age 21
1507 Apr	Ordained priest	Age 23
1508	Lectured at Wittenberg University	Age 24
1510 Nov	Visit to Rome	Age 26
1512 Oct 19	Became doctor at Wittenberg University	Age 28
1516 Oct 31	Dispute about Indulgences	Age 32
1517 Oct 31	Ninety-five Theses	Age 33
1518 Mar	Heidelberg	Age 34
1519	Leipzig	Age 35
1520	Pamphlets published	Age 36
1521 Jan	Book Burning	Age 37

1521 Apr	Excommunicated from church	Age 37
1521 Apr 20	Diet of Worms	Age 37
1521 May 5	Kidnapped	Age 37
1522 Mar	Returned to Wittenberg	Age 38
1524	Peasants' Rebellion	Age 40

1525 Jun 27	Married Katherine von Bora	Age 41
1534	Translation of Old Testament published	Age 50
1546 Feb 18	Died at Eisleben	Age 62

5

THE THUNDERSTORM

As the horse plunged forward, covered with sweat in the hot afternoon, the sky grew blacker and the atmosphere more threatening. Martin, after a short holiday at home, was riding back to Erfurt to the university. He had already gained his university degree and would soon be making his living in the world. Now he shivered suddenly. *"I don't like it! There's something dreadful in the air! It feels like the end of the world!"*

If it *were*, what would happen to him? Not heaven, he wasn't good enough. Surely he was not bad enough to be sent to hell, either! No, it would be purgatory – the place between heaven and hell that the priests were always preaching about...purgatory, where souls stayed for thousands of years, suffering and tormented until God was satisfied. The thought terrified him.

All at once there was an immense crash of thunder, a blinding flash of lightning that made his horse rear up. He was flung to the ground and felt he was dying.

"St. Anne, help me!" he shouted in terror. "If you save me I'll do anything...I promise to become a monk!" The storm passed but the horror of it stayed with Martin as he rode back, shivering, to Erfurt and gathered his student-friends together for a last party. When it was over he walked slowly away from them, hardly saying good-bye. He had made his promise to St. Anne and he could not go back on his word.

Through the monastery gateway he walked up the stone-flagged pathway to the monastery door. He lifted his hand and knocked.

6

"THE CHURCH IS ALWAYS RIGHT!"

It was two years before Martin saw his father again. He had been accepted as a "learner," a novice, for his first year in the monastery, and he found it a harder life than he had ever imagined. He shared in begging for food from the townspeople, since what the monks ate was very little and unappetizing. They kept silence for a great deal of the time, and nearly half of every day was spent praying in the chapel services or in their own small cells. When they were not praying they were at work in the monastery itself, cleaning, cooking, washing, or in the vegetable garden.

There was very little time for study and nothing to stretch the mind of a brilliant young scholar like Martin Luther.

Prior Staupitz, the head of the monastery, watched him growing thinner, more worried, and unhappy. Not even the privations and self-discipline of the monastery left Martin feeling that God would ever be pleased with him.

At the service when he was ordained as a priest, his father watched him anxiously. This was the young man he had hoped would be a wealthy, successful lawyer. After the service he told Martin what he thought.

"The Church has no right to deal with young men like this – making them afraid, leaving them hungry, letting them beg for food!"

Martin's answer was short and sharp. "Father, the Church is always right!"

That was something he would soon change his mind about.

And the wonderful news he was given shortly afterwards by Prior Staupitz would help him do so.

Luther was ordained as a priest in the Augustinian monastery in April 1507.

7

ROME – THE HOLY CITY

"There is to be a great conference of all our Augustinian monasteries and we have to send two monks to represent us," Prior Staupitz told Martin and another young monk. "I have decided to send *you*." He smiled at their astonishment. "You are going to Rome, the holiest city in the world. You may even see the pope himself, the head of the Church."

After walking for many weeks through Germany, Switzerland, and Italy, Luther arrived at Rome, which did not seem very holy at all. Monks looked well fed. Priests were laughing and enjoying themselves with women as well as men. They raced through six services while he was taking one. With the other pilgrims, the two young monks paid to see the astonishing relics in church after church – a thorn from the burning bush that Moses saw; some hairs from the donkey that Jesus rode into Jerusalem, a bit of wood from Christ's Cross. Martin wondered if these things could possibly be real. He climbed the stairs they said Jesus climbed in Pontius Pilate's palace...and wondered if *they* were the real thing.

Nothing was as Martin had thought it would be.

On one occasion he saw a splendid palaquin – a chair carried by half a dozen servants – with a richly dressed man in it, wearing jewels and rings. He must, thought Martin, be one of the great princes of Rome.

A man beside him nudged him. "Down on your knees, monk! Quick! That is His Holiness the Pope!"

St. Peter's church, Rome, begun by
Pope Leo X. Money was raised toward
its cost through the selling of
indulgences.

8

THE NEW PROFESSOR

The road to Rome had been hard going, but lightened by the thrill of what he would find in the wonderful holy city. The long trek back was much harder. Rome's churches, monks, and priests, even the pope himself, had left Martin depressed. So many things had seemed wrong. He must talk to Prior Staupitz when he got back! But somehow he did not open his heart to the prior as he might have done – partly because Staupitz had some other exciting news for him.

The great duke of the state, Frederick the Wise, was enlarging his university in Wittenberg. "More and more students are coming," he had said to Prior Staupitz. "We'll soon be as famous as Leipzig! We need three more professors. Have you got any good young men among your monks in the monastery?"

"I've got one," said the prior. "He's brilliant...was going to be a lawyer...not a very cheerful man but he would make a good teacher. The students would like him – he was *very* popular as a student at Erfurt."

So, Martin, at the age of twenty-eight, though he was still a monk and a priest, became a very popular professor, lecturing on Aristotle and the influence of philosophy on theology, at the great university of Wittenberg.

But two things he could not get out of his mind: the scandalous things he had seen in Rome, and the certainty that God had still not forgiven him for his own sins.

9

"I THOUGHT THE BIBLE WAS DULL!"

Prior Staupitz and Duke Frederick both believed they had chosen
well when they appointed Martin Luther as a professor in the
university, but they were both rather worried about him. He *was*
popular, he understood his students, he was a brilliant teacher.
And yet, though he never explained why, he still seemed worried
and unhappy – even more so since the wonderful opportunity of
visiting Rome. Perhaps, thought Staupitz, he needed the challenge
of even *more* work.

"Brother Martin," he said one day, as they stood under the pear
tree in the garden, "I have too many duties to do them all properly.
I am going to give up my work as 'professor of the Bible.'"

"But," broke in Martin, "you *can't* do that. It's because of your
lectures that so many men come to Wittenberg!"

"I have a very good man to take my place," said Staupitz. "*You*
are to be the new professor of Biblical Studies!"

"*Me!*" Martin almost shouted. "You can't mean that! I hardly
know anything about the Bible...only what we read in the services
in church."

"Then you had better begin to learn about it quickly. The duke
has already appointed you. Get down to the library and start now!"
He smiled as Martin turned away, shaking his head as if someone
had hit him between the eyes.

"The Bible is so *dull*," he muttered to himself as he stood in
front of the great leather-bound, handwritten volumes. "No
wonder no one reads it." They were big, heavy, and all were
written in Latin. He took down one of the New Testament books
and put it on the desk.

S A Y I N G S   O F   L U T H E R

- Stubbornness should have been my middle name.
- We who preach the gospel are a road on which Satan rides.
- When I rest, I rust.
- I comfort myself with the thought that with time my books will remain covered in dust, except where I have written something good.
- A mighty fortress is our God.

- A safe stronghold our God is still, a trusty shield and weapon.
- Our Lord God commonly gives riches to those gross asses to whom He gives nothing else.
- The confidence and faith of the heart alone make both God and me idols.
- The way of the ungodly will perish. But it will endure for a long while yet. So be steadfast.
- There are to be no bond-slaves since Christ has freed us all.
- There is no reason why the Devil should keep all the beautiful melodies for himself.
- Here I stand. I can do no other. God help me. Amen.
- If I had heard that as many devils would set on me in Worms as there are tiles on the roofs, I should, nonetheless, have ridden there.

Martin Luther.

10

MARTIN FINDS OUT THE TRUTH

He could hardly keep away from these great volumes once he started reading them. Why had he never read the Bible before? Why had he thought it would be dull? Every page he read was exciting! Suddenly Jesus seemed to be a real person, and the words He had said came to life. "Whoever believes in me will have eternal life...Go in peace...Your sins are forgiven...God is *love!*" *If God is like Jesus*, thought Martin, *there is no need to be afraid of Him ever again.*

"No one comes to the Father except through *me!*" said Jesus.

"So there is no need to go to the priest to ask for forgiveness. I can go straight to God," Martin said to himself. "And forgiveness is *free*...no need to pay the priest for special services, or to see relics that can't possibly be the real things!" The Book of Romans made it especially clear for him. In chapter 5 verse 1 he read: "Therefore being justified by faith, we have peace with God through our Lord Jesus Christ."

Suddenly all the misery of the years was swept away. God was *not* angry with him; God *loved* him; God would forgive him, always. He was already forgiven, and free.

But if the Bible was right – and he was sure it was, after reading it over and over again – *if the Bible was right, many of the things in the Church must be wrong!* It was a terrible thought for someone who had always believed that everything the Church said and did was *right* but...his mind went back to Rome and the things he had seen.

Just as Martin was making that discovery exciting news began to spread through Germany.

(Over) Tetzel selling indulgences to raise money for the building of St. Peter's church in Rome. It was abuses like this which angered Luther and inspired him to write his "Ninety-five Theses."

11

TETZEL

Martin had already seen the beginnings of the great new cathedral, St. Peter's, in Rome.

The pope was sending a monk named Tetzel throughout the empire with splendid news for everybody. He was already on the borders of the great Duke Frederick's territory, and people came back with vivid descriptions of what he said and did. He had trumpeters and messengers to announce his coming, and then his servants came forward with piles and piles of parchments.

"These," cried Tetzel, "are *indulgences*. You all know that when you die you will not go to heaven or hell but to *purgatory*. And there you will stay, tormented by the devils for thousands of years, until you have paid for all your sins. But these are special indulgences from the pope himself! If you buy these you will get out of purgatory a hundred, even a thousand, years more quickly. It all depends on how much you pay. You can buy them to get your parents or your friends out of purgatory! You can buy them to forgive big sins and little sins! You can even buy one that will get you forgiveness for all the sins you commit between now and the time you die! Come and buy them now! All the money will help to build the great church of St. Peter in Rome."

The crowds surged forward. It seemed there would hardly be enough "indulgences" for all who wanted them!

Now it was clear to Martin where money to build St. Peter's was coming from.

Pope Leo X, who came to power in 1513.

24

12

THE NINETY-FIVE THESES

When Martin heard what Tetzel was preaching and doing – *selling* God's forgiveness – he was shocked and very angry. Everything he had come to believe through reading the Bible proved that neither priests, monks nor even the Pope himself could forgive sins. Only God could do that – and forgiveness was *free* to those who believed.

Duke Frederick, influenced by Martin, refused to allow Tetzel to cross the borders into his territory and when the pope heard this he was furious. But something else that happened in Wittenberg made him more angry still.

Martin always seemed to be busy. At first it was preaching in the monastery church and the duke's town church, looking after eleven other monasteries, even making sure the monastery fish pool was always well-stocked. Later, however, he always seemed to be writing, and on All Saints Day, 1517, the people of Wittenberg *saw* what he had been working on so urgently.

He walked across the square and nailed a great parchment to the church door. The paper contained ninety-five separate statements. They were called "theses" in the university...statements about God, forgiveness, the Bible, indulgences and so on.

"Look at *this*...just read that...Dr. Luther says..." students and other people shouted to each other as they read the paper.

Very soon they were saying: "If what Dr. Luther says is right, then *the Church is wrong*!"

13

"THINGS WILL HAVE TO CHANGE"

It was not only the people in Wittenberg who saw the "Ninety-five theses", nor the university professors and students who argued about them. By this time printing was being used everywhere, and very soon Martin Luther's statements on the church door were being printed and distributed all over Germany. It was not long before they were seen in Rome, too, and what the pope said to his counselors made it clear that Martin was in very real danger. "This man is protesting against all the Church says and does! He must be stopped!"

Now, quite suddenly, it seemed that other thoughtful men were thinking in the same way as Martin. In France and Switzerland as well as Germany, professors and priests were "protesting" and soon those who acted in this way were known as "Protestants." Some of them would leave the Catholic church in the near future and begin churches of their own – the first "Protestant churches."

Martin Luther himself had no wish to leave the Church in which he had grown up. He simply wanted to see it change for the better..."reformed." The pope and the leaders of the Catholic church were determined to get rid of these "reformers" at any cost. The Church would not change. But they could not stop what was happening.

The "Reformation" had begun.

Luther nails his "Ninety-five Theses"
to the church door in Wittenberg.

THE NINETY-FIVE THESES

- Although the Pope could issue a penance, he had no power to commit a soul to purgatory.
- The Pope had the power to release someone from an imposed penance—but not to release a soul from purgatory.
- *If* the Pope had the power to decide a soul's fate, why couldn't he release that soul from purgatory through Christian love rather than money?
- It was the Pope's duty to *pray for* the salvation of souls, not to *sell* it.
- It was also his duty to help people *accept* any punishment imposed by God, not *escape* from it.
- The only way to seek *God's indulgence* was to be truly sorry for one's sins.
- When masses had been paid for to benefit a soul in purgatory and then an Indulgence was bought, wasn't that soul then freed from purgatory? If so, shouldn't the money paid for the masses be returned to the person's family? Why pray for a soul already in heaven?
- The Pope was not king of the Church, merely "supreme pastor of the flock"—*and the flock belonged to God.*

14

"TELL THE WORLD YOU'RE WRONG!"

Despite running away when he was a little boy, and later becoming a monk because of his panic in the storm, Martin had never lacked courage, and now that he was so sure of God's love and strength, his courage was greater than ever. In the next few years he was greatly in need of it.

When he refused the pope's order to go to Rome and stand trial for his "wrong opinions," the pope decided that Martin should stand trial before a cardinal who was visiting Germany. In the great town of Augsburg, just a year after he had nailed his challenges to the church door in Wittenberg, Luther stood quietly in his monk's robes before Cardinal Cajetan.

"Dr. Luther, you have been teaching wrong things!"

"But I can prove from the Bible..." began Luther.

"People are not allowed to read the Bible. It is too dangerous!" snapped the cardinal. "You are not here to argue. *You are here to admit you are wrong!*"

At the next day's hearing the stubborn monk still refused to admit anything of the kind. Cardinal Cajetan stared at him grimly. "I will give you until tomorrow to change your mind." He tapped a roll of parchment in his hand. "If you do not, you know what will happen to you."

Outside the courthouse friendly townspeople called to him, hustled him onto a horse, led him down narrow alleyways and through the town gates of Augsburg into the countryside.

The next day Martin Luther was safely back in Wittenberg.

15

"MARTIN LUTHER SHOULD BE BURNED!"

There were many angry men who were saying more and more loudly, that Martin should be burned, for that was a period when "heretics" – people who denied what the Roman Catholic Church taught – *were* burned to death at the stake, as a warning to the watching crowds. Part of the problem for the ope and his councils was that more and more influential men were also saying what Luther was saying...that the Bible was right and the Church was wrong. John Calvin was saying it in France, and gaining followers. Ulrich Zwingli was saying it in Germany and Switzerland. "Luther is right! The Bible is right! The Church is wrong about purgatory and penance and forgiveness, wrong about what God is like! You don't need priests to forgive your sins! Only God can do that – and *He* does so because He loves us."

The "Protestants" were gaining more and more followers. The "Reformation" was changing people's ideas of God and worship even if it could not for the moment change the Church.

It was no wonder the Pope was angry or that he sent a special letter to Martin Luther telling him he *must* come to Rome.

"If you go you'll be burned to death," said his horrified friends in Wittenberg.

"I've no intention of risking it," said Martin. "I'm not going to Rome. Let's have our own bonfire *here*!" He took the Pope's letter in his hand, and thrust it into the flames. "Let's burn the Pope's letter instead!"

Luther burning the papal bull (an official document from the Pope), which notified him of his excommunication, that his books and he himself were to be burned.

31

16

THE DIET OF WORMS

Worms was an important town in Germany, and the "Diet" was the emperor's council. It was to this "Diet" in the city of Worms that Martin Luther, thirty-seven years old, made his way in 1521. If he would not go to Rome, he must answer for himself in Germany. This time he *must* acknowledge that he was wrong and so bring this dangerous "Reformation" to an end or else "face the consequences" – and that, he knew, meant he would be killed...probably burned. The emperor had promised that he would be safe as he traveled from Wittenberg and returned when the council was over, but very few people really trusted that promise.

Yet, Luther's words as he refused to admit that he was wrong were clear and defiant:

"Here I stand! I can do no other. So help me God!"

The trial before the council lasted four days, some agreeing with Martin Luther, others bitterly opposing. No solution was reached, though after Martin and his supporters had left, the emperor and pope's representative agreed that he would be arrested for heresy and opposing the government.

Martin Luther had been safe enough in Worms, where many of the citizens would have defended him to the death, and he *hoped* he would be safe as he left Worms in the slow-moving cart with other monks from Wittenberg. They trundled through fields and villages into the forest. Then, suddenly, in the deepest gloom of the woods, there were angry shouts. The cart was stopped by mounted horsemen and Luther was dragged out and pushed onto another horse. The whirling, shouting group of horsemen disappeared into the trees.

Luther defending himself at the Diet of Worms in 1521.

33

17

"MARTIN LUTHER IS DEAD!"

From the moment he was abducted from the cart carrying him and his fellow monks back to Wittenberg, Luther disappeared completely. The story the monks told of the terrifying men in the forest horrified most people and puzzled others. There was a shocked feeling of loss. It quickly became clear that Luther was now one of the heroes of the German people. They had lost their most influential leader, and the Protestants in France and Switzerland, too, felt the same.

Most people believed that Luther had been kidnapped by his enemies in the Church and was almost certainly dead. But the Catholic Church leaders were puzzled, too, for they had *not* arranged the abduction.

Luther's kidnappers had ridden, without speaking to him, through the forest to a castle high above the plains and the forests. There, they undid the ropes that bound his hands and thrust him into a room where a man was waiting – a man whom Luther knew well, and liked greatly – a trusted official from duke Frederick's own government. The duke must have turned against him after all!

"I am sorry we had to do it this way," said the duke's man. "It was important that *no one* should know what happened to you. You must disappear until it is safe for you to go back to Wittenberg. This is the Wartburg, one of the duke's own castles, and you will be here for the next few months!"

18

THE PRISONER IN THE WARTBURG

There were times when he felt he really *was* a prisoner, even though he was being kept in the castle for his own safety's sake. "And," as the duke's servant said, "we *have* to keep you safe. Germany can't do without you now!" Neither the servants nor the soldiers knew who he was, and to preserve the secret the monk's robe was put away and he wore the dress of a knight-at-arms. Curly brown hair grew on his shaved head, and he wore a full dark beard.

Slowly, however, the news spread that he was alive after all, as leaflets and pamphlets with his name on them were printed and distributed throughout Germany.

News reached the Wartburg from the world outside, too, and some of it shocked the great reformer. One day he rode out from the castle to Wittenberg. No one recognized the black-bearded knight as he strode into the castle church. His feet scrunched on the broken pieces of a statue and he saw where others had been thrown down. On the walls were roughly scrawled slogans.

"This is not what we stand for...not what God wants! This is still the house of God! How dare you profane it!" He spoke on, angrily, and the people stood and listened astonished. It sounded like Dr. Luther's voice!

Suddenly the bearded knight turned, strode out of the church, mounted his horse and rode away, back to the Wartburg.

Frontispiece of a book by Luther attacking Catholic abuses, showing the Pope as an agent of the Devil. (Over) Luther "kidnapped" on his way back from Worms.

19

THE BOOK FOR THE PEOPLE

As it became clear that Luther was alive – and his angry protest in the Wittenberg church made that quite certain – his friends and followers tried to imagine where he was and what he could be doing with his time. He had always been a busy man – but what was he busy at *now*?

The servants and soldiers in the castle wondered the same thing, for he seemed to do nothing but write. The tables in his castle apartment were covered with papers – thick books in Latin, others in strange letters, which he told them were Greek. On and on he went, writing, crossing out, looking up other books and, of course, praying. "He said he's so busy that he has to spend even *more* time praying," quoted one of the servants in a puzzled tone.

Then, at last, it was done...the thing he had longed to do and never had time to do. Month after month he had been translating the New Testament from the Latin the Church used and the Greek it had first been written in into the ordinary German that everyone in the country could understand.

He had insisted, against the Catholic church's opposition, that everyone ought to be able to read the Bible for themselves. Now, at last, his people would have the New Testament in their own tongue. In time he would translate the Old Testament, too.

His translation of the Bible was Luther's greatest gift to the German people.

20

BACK TO WITTENBERG

At last it seemed safe to leave the Wartburg and return "home." Not that Martin had a home of his own, though he would always be welcome at his parents' house. The university had been his "home" for ten years or more, and he had often thought it was a good thing that monks could *not* get married! If he *had* had a wife and a family, he would never have been able to do all he had done. Certainly he would not have been able to spend almost all his time translating the New Testament into the language of the people.

Back in Wittenberg, welcomed by his friends and by the townspeople, he found his German New Testament was selling as fast as the printers could produce copies. Those who read it were, like Luther himself, certain that what the Church said and did needed to be changed and Martin had hoped that the pope himself would lead the way in reforming it. That had not happened and now the people, even priests and monks, were changing things themselves.

Services were being held in German instead of Latin. There were no more indulgences; no absolution (forgiveness) by the priests; even Duke Frederick's costly collection of relics had been removed.

What was happening in Wittenberg was happening elsewhere, too. In England and Scotland, as much as in Germany, the Reformation was producing new "Protestant churches," giving people new freedom to think for themselves.

21

THE PEASANTS' REBELLION

It was not only in the Church that ordinary people wanted to see things changed. Ever since Martin had spoken out against the monk Tetzel selling his indulgences, a drawing had been appearing on the city walls or chalked on buildings – the drawing of a peasant's shoe. This was the symbol of another sort of revolution. The working people of Germany felt they were denied their proper rights. They were not paid proper wages, were forced to live in shocking conditions, had no chance of doing any better for themselves or their children. One day, they declared, they would take things into their own hands.

Then, at last, in 1524, the "Peasants' Rebellion" broke out, with war between the peasants and the lords and landowners. Because Luther stood aside from it and would not speak up for the peasants, he lost a good deal of his popularity. The people had stood by *him*; why would *he* not stand by *them*?

Luther would not get involved in politics; he was committed to reforming the Church and no more. One unhappy result was that many of his followers left his church and joined other Protestant groups led by other reformers.

A contemporary woodcut of German peasants during the revolt of 1524.

22

OUT OF THE CONVENT

Martin was not the only man who had gone into the monastery and so given up the chance of a very good career. Now, however, Protestants came to believe that being a monk was not a special way to please God, but that a man could *work* to God's glory whatever he was doing. The result was that more and more monks left the monasteries, laid their robes aside, took different jobs and even married and had families.

In the past, young women had been urged to become nuns by their parents who would not then have the expense of "marrying them off." Now, as monks left the monasteries, so more and more nuns left the convents. Some, like the monks, got married. More astonishingly, so did some of the priests.

While Martin was back home visiting his parents, his father talked to him very seriously. "I suppose it's no use expecting you to be a lawyer after all this. You're famous, anyway. But you ought to get married, Martin, like the others are doing. Get yourself a good wife and a nice home. You'll have some children, too. That's what you ought to do."

Martin laughed at the idea.

"I've got too much to do to be a husband! I assure you *I'm* not going to get married!"

23
A STRANGE KIND OF FISH

Leonard Kopp, a prosperous merchant in Wittenberg, had been delivering fish to the convent several miles away for years and this day, when he backed his covered, fish-smelling cart up to the back door of the convent, the strong young nuns heaved the barrels out as usual and into the storeroom. The nuns seemed a little longer than usual in getting last week's empty barrels loaded but at last it was done and the cart clip-clopped homeward.

Back in a quiet part of Wittenberg, Martin Luther was waiting when Kopp drew up, pulled back the covering of the cart and looked at the load inside. Some fish barrels were there – but there were also twelve young nuns. They had written to Luther, asking him to help them escape from the convent because they had come to believe in the Protestant way of looking at religion. It was a dangerous moment. If it could be proved that he had helped them escape, Martin could have been burned at the stake in Catholic territory, though not in Duke Frederick's lands.

Luther and Kopp helped them safely to their homes and in a few months eight were married while three remained in their own homes. The wedding of the twelfth, Katherine von Bora, to a young nobleman at the university, was called off because his family objected.

In the end it was Martin himself who married her, and it seemed as if the whole of Wittenberg turned out to see the wedding.

Katherine von Bora, who married Luther in 1525.

L U T H E R   L E T   L O O S E

- As Kate had predicted, the students eventually produced *Table Talk*—a record of conversations they had held with Dr. Luther.
- At Brussels in July 1523, two monks were burnt at the stake for supporting Luther.
- Rome called Luther The "Beast."
- In England, Henry VIII wrote a lengthy tract saying how wrong Luther was, and the Pope awarded him the title "Defender of the Faith," a title every British sovereign since then has inherited.
- Henry's daughter, Mary Tudor, called Luther a fanatic.

- The English church leaders Cranmer, Latimer, Tyndale and Coverdale sided with Luther and met their deaths. The authorities believed such people were not just mistaken but downright sinful and only death could cleanse them of their wickedness.
- Between 1519 and 1556, 30,000 people perished by "the stake or the scaffold" for their beliefs. Most of them were followers of Luther.
- People sailing to America to live took Luther's teaching with them, and it soon became widespread there.
- Today, the Lutheran church still flourishes and Luther is recognized as one of the greatest leaders the Christian Church has ever known. Almost every reform he wanted, people now agree with.

Henry VIII, king of England, wrote a tract attacking Luther for which the Pope rewarded him. However, Henry himself was a few years later to fight against the authority of the Pope, though out of personal ambition rather than a love of God.

(Clockwise from above) Thomas Cranmer, Hugh Latimer, William Tyndale and Miles Coverdale: English church leaders, who were put to death for agreeing with Luther.

A modern Lutheran church in South Africa.

Luther was forty-one when he married in 1525.

24

SAFELY AT HOME

Both Martin Luther and Kopp had very real fears that they might be caught by their enemies, dragged over the border of the state and burned for abducting the nuns. In the end, nothing happened, and it became just one more adventure to be told and laughed about. Luther himself was safe because he never crossed the frontiers of the state. He was always too busy to travel – writing books, seeing a constant stream of people at home, preaching, lecturing, writing hymns.

For twenty years he enjoyed his life with Katherine, though she found it less easy than he did. In the beginning they had no money and their friends had to help them. Then, when money from Martin's writings *did* come in, unless Kate got hold of it first, Martin would give it away to the poor. After a few years there were six children, and the house always seemed to be full – students, visitors from Germany and other countries, old friends, all wanted to talk to the great reformer.

Slowly he grew more tired and less well, but he could never stop writing. His most important writing in these years was his translation of the Old Testament. At last "Luther's Bible" became the best-selling and most read book in Germany. Protestant churches were found everywhere, the Bible was becoming available to people in their own languages and, at last, the Catholic Church was beginning to change.

25
"A SAFE STRONGHOLD"

Though Martin was happy with his family and his friends around him in the last years of his life, he was often ill, slept badly, and had long periods of depression. And yet for most of the time he was good company, cheerful anongst his friends, loving with Kate and his children, and especially enjoyed music.

All heroes are sometimes lonely, and Martin was a true hero. He had had the courage to defy the Church, the pope, and Emperor for what he believed to be the truth. He had driven the Catholic Church to get rid of many of the evils about which he had protested, and he stood firmly for religious liberty. Ever since he had first discovered the Bible for himself, his faith in God and his love for Jesus had sustained him. It was this faith in God that he put into that most famous hymn that he wrote a few years after he was married. *Ein feste Burg*, it began, and it was soon sung all over Germany. Indeed, it is still sung all over the world, especially when the Church is under pressure.

> A safe stronghold our God is still,
> A trusty shield and weapon;
> He'll help us clear from all the ill
> That hath us now o'ertaken.

In 1546 Martin Luther, one of the greatest heroes of the cross, died – but what he did and believed has lived on through the centuries.